EYE to EYE with ANIMALS

MARVELOUS MARINE MAMMALS

by Ruth Owen

WINDMILL BOOKS

New York

Published in 2013 by Windmill Books, An Imprint of Rosen Publishing
29 East 21st Street, New York, NY 10010

Produced for Windmill by Ruby Tuesday Books Ltd
Editor for Ruby Tuesday Books Ltd: Mark J. Sachner
US Editor: Sara Antill
Designer: Emma Randall

Photo Credits:
Cover, 1, 4–5, 11, 12–13, 15, 16 (bottom), 17, 19, 20–21, 23, 25, 27, 28 © Shutterstock; 7, 8–9, 24, 29 © FLPA; 16 (top) © Creative Commons Wikipedia.

Library of Congress Cataloging-in-Publication Data

Owen, Ruth, 1967–
 Marvelous marine mammals / by Ruth Owen.
    p. cm. — (Eye to eye with animals)
 Includes index.
 ISBN 978-1-4488-8070-6 (library binding) — ISBN 978-1-4488-8106-2 (pbk.) — ISBN 978-1-4488-8112-3 (6-pack)
 1. Marine mammals—Juvenile literature. I. Title.
 QL713.2.O94 2013
 599.5—dc23
                                    2012009785

Manufactured in the United States of America

CPSIA Compliance Information: Batch # B2S12WM: For Further Information contact Windmill Books, New York, New York at 1-866-478-0556

CONTENTS

Meet the Marine Mammals!

They live in the ocean, some have blubber to keep them warm, they love to eat seafood, and they are excellent swimmers. Meet the marine mammals!

Mammals are warm-blooded animals with backbones that give birth to live young and feed them with milk from their bodies. Marine mammals are **species** that spend all of their time, or a large part of their time, in the water. Just like land mammals, and unlike fish, these animals must regularly come to the water's surface to breathe air.

Two bottlenose dolphins

In this book you will meet the largest animal ever to have lived on Earth, one of the smartest animals on Earth, skillful hunters, and gentle plant-eaters. So take a deep breath, dive in, and let's go eye to eye with some of the world's most interesting marine mammals.

An orca

MARINE MAMMALS IN DANGER

Sadly, just like many land mammal species, many marine mammals are **endangered**. Humans have hunted some species almost to **extinction**. For many marine mammals, the future looks uncertain as their ocean **habitat** becomes polluted by chemicals, oil, and **sewage**.

BLUE WHALES
The Largest Animals Ever!

Length: Up to 90 feet (27 m)

Weight: Up to 200 tons (186 t)

Weight at birth: 4,400 pounds (1,996 kg)

Lifespan: Up to 90 years

Breeding age (females): 5 years

Breeding age (males): 5 years

Diet: 3 to 4 tons (2.7–3.5 t) of tiny shellfish, called krill, each day

Habitat: All the world's oceans

FACE FACTS

A blue whale eats by gulping up huge quantities of water that contains **krill**. Inside its mouth, the whale has stiff filters called baleen plates, which are made of keratin (the stuff that fingernails are made of). The whale flushes the water out through its baleen plates and the krill gets trapped in the plates. Then the whale swallows the tiny animals.

A blue whale surfaces to breathe.

7

ORCAS
Killer Whales

Length: **Up to 32 feet (9.75 m)**

Weight: **Up to 15,900 pounds (7,200 kg)**

Weight at birth: **300 pounds (136 kg)**

Lifespan: **36 to 65 years**

Breeding age (females): **15 years**

Breeding age (males): **10 to 13 years**

Diet: **Prey such as smaller whales, dolphins, sharks, seals, sea lions, walruses, sea otters, fish, squid, octopuses, sea turtles, sea birds**

Habitat: **All the world's oceans, including cold seas in the Arctic and Antarctic**

FACE FACTS

An adult orca can eat up to 100 pounds (45 kg) of food a day. An orca usually tears up large **prey** before eating it, but its throat is large enough to swallow small walruses and seals whole!

Orcas are whales that live in family groups called pods.

Teamwork

The members of an orca pod will sometimes hunt as a team. They may catch a seal that's resting on an **ice floe** by swimming together to create a big wave that washes the seal into the water. They may also encircle a larger whale of a different species and take turns attacking the animal.

Family Life

A female orca gives birth to a single calf that measures up to 8 feet (2.4 m) long. She feeds the calf milk for up to a year. The calf feeds for about 10 seconds at a time as its mother slowly glides through the water.

An orca stays with its mother's pod for its whole life. It learns hunting skills from its mother and other older pod members, and young females learn how to raise calves.

A female orca and her calf

An orca pod

12

An orca leaps from the water and then splashes back down. This is called breaching.

The Future for Orcas
Unlike many whale species, orcas have not been hunted by humans in large numbers.

In the future, threats to orcas include pollution of their ocean habitat by chemicals and oil spills. Pollution also damages the orcas' prey.

Whale watching boat trips help teach people about orcas. Some scientists are concerned, however, that the number of whale-watching boats in certain areas may disturb the orcas too much and force pods to leave places where they have always lived.

ORCAS RANGE MAP

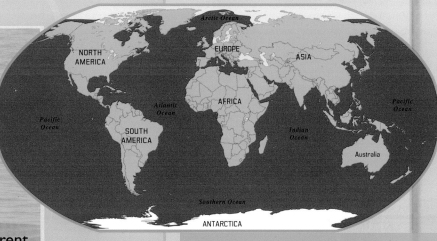

The red areas on the map show where orcas live wild.

TALKING ORCA

Orcas communicate using whistles, calls, and clicking noises. Each pod has its own version of orca language, in the way that people from different parts of the same country may have their own accent and use different words to mean the same thing.

BOTTLENOSE DOLPHINS
Smart Marine Mammals

Length: Up to 12.5 feet (3.8 m)

Weight: 550 to 1,100 pounds (250–500 kg)

Weight at birth: Up to 44 pounds (20 kg)

Lifespan: 25 to 50 years

Breeding age (females): 10 years

Breeding age (males): 13 to 20 years

Diet: Fish, squid, shrimp

Habitat: Warm oceans around the world

FACE FACTS

There are many different types of dolphins. The best known is the smiley-faced bottlenose dolphin. A dolphin breathes by swimming to the water's surface and opening and closing the blowhole on top of its head.

Adult bottlenose dolphin

Dolphins live in groups called schools. A school may have just two members, or as many as a thousand members!

Hunting With Sound

A dolphin hunts its prey using **echolocation**. It sends out clicking noises from the rounded, fatty part of its forehead. When the sound hits a fish, the click bounces back to the dolphin as an echo, which the dolphin picks up through its lower jaw. The echo tells the dolphin the fish's size, its shape, its speed, and how far away it is.

Dolphin Calves

A female bottlenose dolphin gives birth to a single calf, which she feeds with milk. A mother dolphin cares for her calf for up to five years.

Female dolphins form nursery schools so they can help each other care for their babies. A calf's grandmother or older sister will sometimes babysit for it, too,

An adult female bottlenose dolphin with two young dolphins

A school of dolphins

16

SUPER SMART DOLPHINS

Dolphins sometimes work as a team to encircle a school of fish and force them into a big ball. Then they can easily grab mouthfuls. Scientists have taught some dolphins to recognize human words. Smart dolphins have even been known to protect humans from sharks, and help a drowning boy by pushing him to a boat!

Dangers to Dolphins

Dolphins are in danger from pollution and fishing boats.

Dolphins can be harmed by pollution in the ocean such as oil spills, chemicals, and sewage.

Dolphins can become trapped underwater in fishing nets and drown. Seafood that is marked "dolphin friendly" has been caught using fishing methods that do not endanger dolphins.

In some areas people catch so many fish there are not enough left for dolphins to eat.

BOTTLENOSE DOLPHINS RANGE MAP

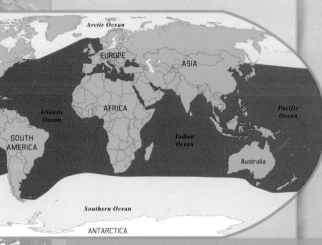

The red areas on the map show where bottlenose dolphins live wild.

Scientists think that dolphins sometimes leap from the water to send each other messages such as "let's go!"

17

SEA LIONS
Marine Mammals
That Roar!

Length: 4 to 11 feet (1.2–3.4 m) depending on species

Weight: 110 to 2,200 pounds (50–1,000 kg) depending on species

Weight at birth: 13 to 49 pounds (6–22 kg) depending on species

Lifespan: 20 to 30 years

Breeding age (females): 3 to 8 years

Breeding age (males): 6 to 10 years

Diet: Fish, squid, crabs, and clams; Steller sea lions (the largest species) also eat seals

Habitat: Oceans and rocky shorelines

FACE FACTS

It can be difficult to tell seals and sea lions apart. One important difference is that sea lions have little ear flaps, while seals only have ear holes. When a sea lion is diving to find food, its nostrils automatically close up. It can stay underwater for 40 minutes!

Adult sea lion

19

Sea lions don't mind hanging out in huge groups!
When they gather together on land, a sea lion group
is called a colony.

A bull sea lion keeps watch over his cows.
Bulls are much larger than cows.

The Life of a Bull

During the breeding season, each bull, or male, sea lion tries to gather together a group of about 15 cows, or females, to **mate** with. He then protects his cows to stop other males from stealing them away! The places where sea lions gather to mate and have their pups are known as rookeries.

A colony of sea lions resting on a pier

KEEP THE NOISE DOWN!

Bull sea lions roar, bark, and honk loudly to tell other males to stay away from their females. Female sea lions bark, too, and pups make a bleating noise. If a pup gets separated from its mother, it can recognize her bark among the hundreds of other barks in a rookery.

Mothers and Pups

A female sea lion gives birth to her pup on land. The pup drinks its mother's milk. The fatty milk soon helps the pup grow the layer of blubber it needs to stay warm in the sea.

Mother sea lions teach their pups how to swim and how to hunt for fish. The young sea lions must also learn how to escape from **predators**, such as sharks and orcas!

A three-month-old sea lion pup

Endangered Sea Lions

There are six different species of sea lions. Steller sea lions, Australian sea lions, and Galapagos sea lions are endangered.

Before changes were made to fishing gear in the early 1980s, thousands of Steller sea lions in Alaska were killed because they became trapped in fishing nets and drowned.

Sea lions and fishermen are in competition for the same food. Some fishermen think of sea lions as pests and shoot them.

SEA LION RANGE MAP

The red areas on the map show where sea lions live wild.

21

HARP SEALS
White Coats

Length: Up to 6.5 feet (2 m)

Weight: Up to 300 pounds (136 kg)

Weight at birth: 23 pounds (10.5 kg)

Lifespan: 20 to 35 years

Breeding age (females): 10 years

Breeding age (males): 8 years

Diet: Fish and shellfish

Habitat: Arctic Ocean and northern Atlantic Ocean

FACE FACTS

Harp seal pups are born with a coat of white fur that gives the pups their nickname of "white coats." The white fur is known as lanugo. When a pup is about 21 days old, it begins to lose its lanugo. The white fur is replaced by a silvery coat covered with black spots.

A harp seal pup, or "white coat"

23

Adult harp seals spend most of their time alone in the ocean.

Harp Seal Life

A harp seal may swim up to 3,000 miles (4,800 km) in a year traveling from hunting places to the area where it mates and back again.

Harp Seal Pups

A female harp seal gives birth to a single pup on the ice. She feeds the pup milk from her body. When the mother seal goes hunting, the pup waits on the ice near the hole where its mother enters and leaves the water.

A newborn pup waits on the ice while its mother goes to hunt.

A mother harp seal feeds her baby for 10 to 12 days. Then she abandons the pup on the ice. The pup waits alone until its baby fur is gone and its silver fur has grown in. This is a dangerous time and many pups are killed by polar bears. After about four weeks the pup is ready to enter the ocean and begin hunting for fish.

A young harp seal with a silver coat and black spots

BABY FAT

A mother harp seal's milk is very fatty. In the 10 to 12 days that the pup feeds from its mother, it gains about 70 pounds (32 kg) in weight!

The Future for Harp Seals
At the present time, harp seals are not in danger.

Harp seals have been hunted throughout history for their fur and meat. Hunting of these seals continues today, but the high numbers of these animals means they are not threatened.

In Canada, tourists can visit the areas where harp seal pups are born. This has become an important part of the tourism industry for Canada.

HARP SEAL RANGE MAP

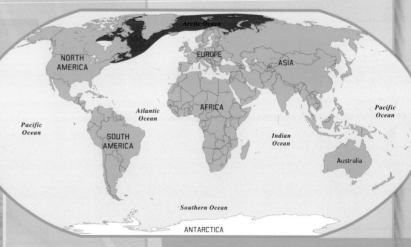

The red areas on the map show where harp seals live wild.

A harp seal pup drinks milk from its mother.

WEST INDIAN MANATEES

Sea Cows

Length: Up to 15 feet (4.5 m)

Weight: 880 pounds (400 kg) average weight

Weight at birth: 66 pounds (30 kg)

Lifespan: 30 years

Breeding age (females): 4 to 5 years

Breeding age (males): 9 to 10 years

Diet: Sea grasses and other water plants

Habitat: Shallow coastal waters and sometimes in estuaries (the places where rivers meet oceans), rivers, and canals.

FACE FACTS

The West Indian manatee has a split upper lip that helps it to move plants into its mouth. The rough plants these animals eat wear down their molars (large, grinding teeth), so they grow new molars throughout their whole lives.

Adult West Indian manatee

27

Adult manatees sometimes live alone, and sometimes spend time with other manatees.

The Life of a Manatee

Manatees feed and are active day and night. When it's time for a break, they rest on the seabed. A resting manatee must rise to the surface every few minutes, however, to take a breath of air.

The plants that manatees eat do not contain many **nutrients** so these large animals have to eat a lot! An adult manatee may graze for up to 8 hours a day and eat 220 pounds (100 kg) of grass and plants in that time.

A manatee calf drinking milk from its mother

An adult manatee feeding on plants

Manatee Calves

A female manatee gives birth to a single calf. The newborn manatee can measure up to 4.5 feet (1.4 m) long. The calf drinks milk from its mother, but also starts to eat plants when it is about three weeks old. A mother manatee takes care of her calf for around two years.

UNDERWATER GYMNASTS

Manatees may look large and lumbering, but they can actually be very acrobatic. Manatees perform rolls, somersaults, and will even swim upside down!

Manatees In Danger

Manatees have no predators except for humans.

Throughout history, manatees were hunted for their meat and skins. Today, many laws are in place to protect manatees. In some places, however, people break the law and still kill these animals.

Manatees sometimes become entangled in fishing nets and drown. They are also killed by motorboats.

Manatees are in danger from chemicals and other pollution that can harm the animals and the plants they feed on.

WEST INDIAN MANATEE RANGE MAP

The red areas on the map show where West Indian manatees live wild.

GLOSSARY

blubber (BLUH-ber)
Thick fat that keeps animals living in the ocean or in cold places warm.

communicate (kuh-MYOO-nih-kayt)
To share facts or feelings.

decibels (DEH-sih-belz)
Units of measurement used to measure the volume of sounds. Silence is measured as 0 decibels, while a gunshot is 140 decibels.

echolocation (eh-koh-loh-KAY-shun)
One way that a dolphin collects information about its environment. A dolphin sends out sounds that bounce off objects such as fish, predators, and rocks. When the sounds, or echoes, travel back to the dolphin, it uses them to create a picture of things it cannot see with its eyes.

endangered (in-DAYN-jerd)
In danger of no longer existing.

extinction (ek-STINGK-shun)
No longer existing.

habitat (HA-buh-tat)
The place where an animal or plant normally lives. A habitat may be a rain forest, the ocean, or a backyard.

ice floe (EYES FLOH)
A sheet or large chunk of floating ice.

krill (KRIL)
Tiny, ocean-living, shrimplike shellfish.

mammal (MA-mul)
A warm-blooded animal that has a backbone and usually has hair, breathes air, and feeds milk to its young.

mate (MAYT)
An animal's partner with which it has young; when a male and a female come together in order to have young.

nutrients (NOO-tree-ents)
Substances that a body needs to help it live and grow. Plants and other foods contain nutrients such as vitamins.

predators (PREH-duh-terz)
Animals that hunt and kill other animals for food.

prey (PRAY)
An animal that is hunted by another animal as food.

sewage (SOO-ij)
Human waste.

species (SPEE-sheez)
One type of living thing. The members of a species look alike and can produce young together.

Websites

For web resources related to the subject of this book, go to: www.windmillbooks.com/weblinks and select this book's title.

READ MORE

King, Zelda. *Manatees*. Marine Mammals. New York: PowerKids Press, 2012.

Metz, Lorijo. *Discovering Sea Lions*. Along the Shore. New York: PowerKids Press, 2012.

Nicklin, Flip, and Linda Nicklin. *Face to Face with Dolphins*. Face to Face with Animals. Des Moines, IA: National Geographic Children's Books, 2010.

Royston, Angela. *Blue Whales*. Amazing Animals. New York: Weigl Publishing, 2010.

INDEX